The answers
are always in your boat.
Keep paddlin' on —

Reflections from the
Red Kayak

Thoughts on Life

by
Mary Anne Smrz

An NBCS, Inc. Production

email: ~~info@redkayakinstitute.org~~ *info @ Red Kayah - Net*
Website: ~~www.redkayakinstitute.org~~ *Red kayah. Net*

Reflections from the Red Kayak, Third Edition

Published in the United States by Pearl editions, LLC.

Design and layout by Josette Songco.
Photographs by Mary Anne Smrz, unless otherwise noted.
Printed in the United States of America.

ISBN 978-0-9832426-4-2

The purpose of this book is to inspire and comfort. The
information is designed to acquaint individuals with the process
of journaling as a way to gain insight. neither the author nor the
publisher is engaged in rendering medical or counseling advice.
If such advice is required, the services of a qualified medical
professional should be sought. The author and publisher shall not
be held liable or responsible to any person or entity with respect
to any loss or damage caused or alleged to be caused, directly or
indirectly by the information contained in this publication.

1. Diaries-Authorship. 2. Journals-Authorship. 3. Journal Writing
4. Kayaking 5. Nature Journaling 6. Mind-body Connections

To "Mary" Jan Malloy,
my paddling partner.
Your spirit and
your memory
will always be with me.

Table of Contents

Acknowledgements

I would first like to acknowledge a group of very special friends, who pitched in and bought my first little red kayak for my 40th birthday. What a surprise to come home, open my garage door and find my new vessel of freedom tied with a big beautiful bow. I always wanted to kayak, knowing that I would enjoy being on the water. They gave me a gift beyond measure, and to them I will be ever grateful: Jan Malloy, Bev Oliver, Betsy Oliver, "Ma" Oliver, Janie Ford, Kathy Macneil, Jill Cebrzynski, Mary Kerr, Madelyn Herbert and Mary Malpede.

In gratitude to Dave Jovanovic, my first writing mentor, who taught me the beauty of disciplined writing and encouraged me to keep growing and perfecting this challenging craft. In his memory, my humble words emerge to encourage others to believe in themselves, as he did for me.

I thank my dear friend, Ann Moss, who helped me craft and shape this book during our morning coffees at the "ashram." I treasure your thoughtful insights, impressive creativity and most of all your unending support.

I extend my thanks to my instructor and classmates in the Gotham Writers' Workshop Non-Fiction Writing Class. Without their insightful comments and helpful criticism, and the "knowing" that I had a responsibility to participate with my writing, this project would have stayed on my "to do" list forever.

With gratitude I also acknowledge my special paddling buddies—Mary LaVine, Deb Maschmeier, Janie Ford,

Pat Stejskal, Nancy Cassell, Ken, Joanne, Jake and Nick Steichmann—with whom I shared many wonderful kayaking adventures that enriched my insights and brought me great joy. I look forward to our every excursion on the water.

Special thanks to Josette Songco, my newest paddling buddy and designer of this book. I treasure your friendship, and your creative touches to this book are invaluable. Thank you for always keeping me focused on the "call of my soul."

My deepest appreciation goes to Georgiann Baldino, my friend, colleague, editor and publisher, who came into my life at a time when unexpected change surfaced in both our lives. Thank you for helping me seriously commit to putting these thoughts down on paper. Your own journey as a published author helped me to navigate this process and make this book a reality.

My heartfelt thanks to Joan Anderson and the Wild Women of Whidbey—our retreat together on Whidbey Island helped unlock my desire to continue on with this project and move me forward at a critical turning point in my life.

I am grateful to my sister and her family, Janet, Mark, Dan and Matt Murawski, my brother and sister-in-law, Mike and Diana Smrz, my Aunt Stef and Uncle Jake and all the members of the Borowski, Drogosz and Haraf families, both living and deceased. All of our great moments "up north" were truly an inspiration to me.

Above all, I am grateful to my parents, Rudy and Toni Smrz. To my Mom, for always encouraging my creative side and giving me opportunities to explore my talents from early on. From oil painting to organ lessons, you planted the seeds of creativity within me. To my Dad, whose love of the outdoors took our family to northern Wisconsin when I was very young. His spirit resonates in my heart every time I am in nature. To have finished writing this book on the anniversary of his 83rd birthday keeps me connected to him in a very special way.

Finally, I am deeply indebted to Jan Malloy and Kathy MacNeil, for being a special part of my life during their short time here on earth. Their untimely deaths from cancer taught me that life is too short to put off doing the things I want to do. There are no "somedays," only today.

Mary Anne Smrz
October, 2010

"Live the life you have imagined."

- Henry David Thoreau

Becoming "of the water"

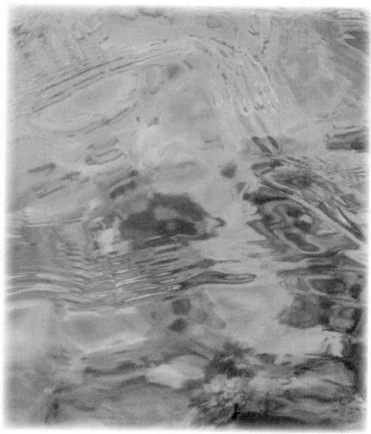

The Great Bay in the Caribbean, St. Thomas, Virgin Islands

Becoming "of the water"

I have always been a "do-er." I see life as a giant "to-do" list, and I am happiest when I am rolling along, checking things off my list. Finish that list. Start a new one. The longer the better. It wasn't until I went onto the water in my red kayak that I learned something new. To take a sabbatical from to-do lists and just "be."

In her book, *Ice Bound,* Dr. Jerry Nielsen writes about her time at the Amundsen-Scott South Pole Station on Antarctica, the most remote and perilous place on earth. She was solely responsible for the health of everyone at the Pole until she was diagnosed with breast cancer, and everyone else became responsible for her. In her account of her experience, she talks about becoming "of the ice." That mixed feeling of both isolation and connectedness, combined with the resolve that she would rather be on Antarctica than anywhere else on earth.

In my kayak, I become öf the water."I have the wonderful feeling of isolation, paddling alone in many places of incredible silence and solitude. I have the complete and overwhelming feeling of oneness with nature and a connectedness to all living things. Gradually I learned I would rather be paddling on the water than be anywhere else in the world.

I also learned that many other people share these feelings of reverence. In the august, 2010 issue of *Canoe and Kayak Magazine,* Mark Jenkins wrote a great article entitled, "The Revivalist." It is the story of Maligiaq Padilla, who he dubs "perhaps the greatest sea kayaker in the world." The story is about Padilla's attempt to revive kayaking in Greenland. At first, this struck me as odd—someone needed to revive kayaking in the land of the Inuit culture where it all began? How could this be? Jenkins wrote, "...a generation ago kayaking had almost died out in Greenland." Kayaking was essential to the life and survival of the Greenland Inuit for over 2000 years. In this article Jenkins also explains some of the deepest, oldest connections people have to the water. He explained that the Inuit hunted seals, walruses and whales by kayak in the summer. "The kayak became the conveyance of human survival, and great hunters were necessarily great kayakers."

As I pondered that thought, my peaceful paddling moments took on greater meaning. I now recognize that kayaking has found its place in my own survival. Certainly not out hunting seals for sustenance, but the realization that the very essence of paddling and time on the water is essential for the survival of my spirit.

My fellow paddlers echo similar sentiments. We may not be kayaking for our physical survival, but we are paddling for something deeper, something within. Away from the speed of everyday life, we slow down, we quiet down and we listen. We are paddling for the survival of our souls.

Which brings me to the premise of this book. The combination of kayaking and journaling for fifteen years has led me to some wonderful analogies of paddling and life. So it is from different trips in my kayak that I share these thoughts with you. The blank pages provide space for your own insights as you paddle. Take time to capture the moments of majesty, awe, and peace, even though you feel the impressions so strongly that it seems they will stay with you forever. Over time those memories may fade or change. Use this journal to capture a moment-to-moment adventure, a tiny spark of nature's glory, or whatever inspires you. Months later you will enjoy returning to the raw experiences. years later these pages will bring back feelings that otherwise would have been lost. My intent is not to fill these pages with my words, but to share my musings, that they may spark some insights of your own. That you, too, may become "of the water."

Simplicity

Atlantic Ocean, Naples, Florida

Simplicity

"All great truths are simple in final analysis
and easily understood;
If they are not, they are not great truths."

~ Napolean Hill

This is a simple book about a simple kayak. The words are uncomplicated and easy to understand. Anyone who paddles knows simplicity is what kayaking is all about.

My first, and most liberating kayaking revelation, is how easily and quickly I am able to get myself on the water. I simply get in the boat and head out. Unlike other boats, there are no covers to remove, no motors to start, no sails to hoist—just me, my paddle and my kayak. Pretty simple. Love it. My next refreshing discovery is how little room exists for excess baggage. I look inside the kayak, which has two small hulls for storage, and quickly realize how simple my journey must be. Without a lot of room for unnecessary things, I can only take what I need and leave the rest behind.

My early morning paddling excursions always entail the core necessities: first aid kit, my compass and whistle safely clipped to my life jacket. The more "frivolous" essentials that go with me are a camera, my journal, a chocolate energy bar and a strong cup of freshly-brewed coffee.

Longer paddling excursions require filling my dry bag, that wonderfully waterproof gallon-sized "suitcase," with more necessities. But even with these additional essentials, the feeling of dipping my paddle end over end into the water, knowing I have very little with me, opens a space inside that longs for less. The experience of simplicity—that basic, uncomplicated, naked truth within—comes bubbling to the surface.

Kayaking allows me to let go. The utter simplicity of getting on the water—put my life jacket on, get my paddle in hand and go—takes me back to a time when life was not so complicated. yearning for simplicity tugs at my inner core and causes me to reevaluate my life from a new perspective and begs the answers to the questions—what do I really need? How can I bring my life back to "simple?"

Many books have been written about simplicity, about letting go of the "baggage" in our lives and lightening our load. In the simplicity of my kayak, I realize a basic lesson—I cant take much with me. I must give some serious thought to what I need to have with me and recognize that the rest is optional.

This "excess baggage" concept got me thinking about life in general. How we stuff our houses with possessions; how we busy our lives always "doing;" how we carry around old emotions that serve no purpose; how we cling to relationships that no longer nourish our growth; how we hold on ... and hold on ...

Our material world, with all its advertisements and promotions, communicates the message that success is defined by what we have, and having more equates to being highly successful. Kayaking teaches me that life can be successful by its sheer simplicity. From the cockpit of my kayak, I can enjoy more natural beauty, experience more inner serenity, and peacefully go to places on the water where no other boats can go, silently, slowly, "one" with the water. Paddling ushers forth the internal rhythm of success on my own terms.

The on-going challenge is to keep that experience of utter simplicity in my daily life. Staying on the path to simplicity requires the continual tedious process of unveiling layers and layers of my life's "stuff," recognizing what serves me and discarding the rest.

This passage to less is very scary. It is extremely unsettling. And yet it is wildly liberating. Bringing simplicity back into my life is one of the most freeing exercises on my personal growth journey.

For me the simplicity of kayaking reinforces the inherent knowing that I am solely responsible for the "stuff" in my life—all of it. Any baggage I take with me is of my own doing. The best part of this catharsis is having the choice on what to keep and what to let go.

And so the questions beg to be answered:

- *What's inside your boat that does not belong?*

- *What are you carrying that no longer serves you?*

- *What thoughts, emotions, people or feelings are a little worn around the edges?*

- *What one thing can you do today to bring simplicity to your life?*

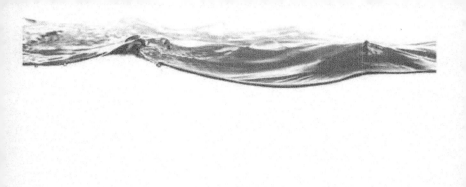

Balance

Wild Rice Lake, Wisconsin

Balance

"There is no secret to balance.
You just have to feel the waves."
- Frank Herbert

There is a known truth about a kayak. If an empty kayak heads down the most forceful of rivers, the sleek little boat will always remain upright. On its own, the kayak will maintain the proper balance necessary to stay afloat. Put a paddler in the craft, and the entire equilibrium changes. It is we, the paddlers, who cause a kayak to flip over by not maintaining our sense of balance.

After a kayaking trip down the gently flowing White Sand River in northern Wisconsin, my younger cousin Jake can tell you all about balance. He paddled so aggressively, he lost his balance and dumped into water. Even though the meandering river was tranquil, he panicked. The capsized boat quickly filled with water, and it took a while for him to calm down and stop struggling. Heavy marsh and high weeds surrounded us, and no shoreline was available for recovery. While we attempted our first on-water kayak rescue, righting his boat and draining out the water, he had to patiently clutch his life jacket and stay afloat. After that unexpected episode, his paddling strokes were more steady and balanced for the remainder of the trip.

On my next trip with Jake and his family the following year, I approached the take out on the calm river and tried to step onto the bank too soon. The kayak drifted and made the exit larger, and I lost my balance. Jake saw what was happening and declared, 'She's going down!"and in that moment, when I took my turn in the river, we shared the same valuable lesson — we are always vulnerable when we lose our sense of balance.

In a kayak the center of gravity is lower, lending itself to more stability. However, sitting in the vessel so close to the water creates a certain sense of instability. The slightest unanticipated motion or sudden disturbance can cause a loss of balance. As Mary Alice Monroe writes in her book, *The Beach House,* "Traveling so near to the water, everything is closer, more immediate." When I first began paddling, I would become startled when a fish unexpectedly jumped nearby, feeling the drops of water splash me as it flipped so near to my kayak. But with each kayaking excursion, I have learned to get closer to that inner peace and balance. Unanticipated occurrences that rattled me before are easier to accept without shaking my inner core. In an almost ironic way, paddling in my kayak on the water "grounds" me.

Kayaking provides many life lessons. Holding the paddle with arms about shoulder length apart is the best position for maximum paddling efficiency. Placing the paddle evenly in the water on both sides of the kayak provides balanced power. Keeping the upper body balanced minimizes the possibility of tipping over. remembering these techniques seems overwhelming, but with each stroke, the natural ease and ebb and flow of paddling emerges. Thoughts no longer focus on proper technique and shift to moving effortlessly on the water.

When I paddle on an open ocean or lake, I know that waves of any size can throw me off balance. Sometimes, the waves are caused by the winds of nature, either gently lapping the water at the side of my kayak, or blowing so fiercely that I can barely maintain control. Often, the waves are caused by other boats, creating a man-made challenge to stay afloat.

In either case, I cannot control the waves, but I can control my response. When the waves come toward me, there are only two choices to make. I can either face the kayak toward these billows meeting them head on, or position my kayak to roll along harmoniously with each swell.

So too, with life's challenges that come our way. Sometimes, we face the adversity head on. Other times, we go with the flow and gently roll along. In every circumstance, the key to effortlessly manage ourselves through these temporary "waves" is to stay centered and balanced, knowing that every menacing whitecap and each gentle ripple has something to teach those of us who are willing to learn.

Every excursion on the water becomes a subtle reminder of the importance of keeping ourselves in balance at all times, even in the calmest waters of our lives. From time to time, we all feel a little out of balance with events, circumstances and people in our lives. Sometimes we come close to tipping over, letting our emotions spill out of control. Sometimes we ourselves dump in, going overboard and overreacting to seemingly insignificant occurrences. Our challenge is to maintain a sense of quiet and order within, so we can effectively handle the swirling state of affairs that we call our lives.

Paddling along, another realization becomes clear. The outer balance of nature is constantly shifting. The speed and direction of the wind, the current in the water, and the unpredictable weather are always in a state of flux. This shifting balance of nature reminds us that our life circumstances, too, are always fluctuating. Balancing the responsibilities of home, work, family, friends, health, finances and so much more is an ever-changing, ever-evolving process. Every day we are tested to find our own natural rhythm, our instinctive balance to handle the shifting occurrences of our lives.

Think about your own life.

- *What is the biggest part of you that is out of balance?*

- *What one thing can you do today to bring yourself closer to a natural rhythm?*

- *How would your life look three years from now if every aspect came into balance?*

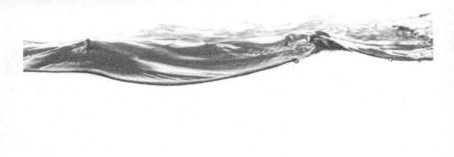

Focus

Penobscot Bay, Maine

Focus

*"As you think,
so shall you be."*

- Dr. Wayne Dyer

There are times in my little red kayak that I feel very focused. I am concentrating on my paddling, intent on keeping my kayak going in a straight direction and very aware of the task at hand. It's usually when I have a bigger purpose, such as paddling across the lake as quickly as possible, that I feel the power of focus within me.

And then sometimes, I have absolutely no focus, no intention other than to go out and paddle. I get this disease I call "around-the-bend-itis," which I define as the urge to aimlessly meander down a winding river, content to paddle no further than just to see what's around the next bend. no purpose, no hurry, no focus.

For me, both types of trips are gifts from heaven. When I have a focus, a purpose to my trip, I feel a great sense of accomplishment at the end. I enjoy beautiful scenery and experience the many wonders of nature along the way as well as attain my goal. When I get, "the disease," a wonderful trip also emerges because along with appreciating the beauty around me, my mind opens to reflective thinking. When I'm not focused on a specific purpose, like getting across the lake quickly, my mind becomes more receptive to hidden thoughts and unclaimed ideas and, without expecting it, the experience provides unforeseen clarity.

And isn't that really what "bringing things into focus"

is, an adjustment for distinctiveness and clarity?

So I learn when I paddle that both types of trips provide a converging point for me because they help me focus in different ways. And both are important. Both provide me with a road map, or "nautical map," if you will, to define my path.

If I am paddling quickly to a designated spot, I am on the path of least resistance and the shortest path "as the crow flies." If I am slowly meandering, I traverse the river from shore to shore, exploring, being inquisitive and taking a closer look at the hidden treasures and unique wonders of nature on the river bank.

I equate both paddling paths to the way we focus in our lives. Our purpose, our bigger vision in our lives, is grounded in our highest values. It is our sense of purpose at a deeper level of being that drives us. Focusing on a mission gives our lives meaning and creates our lasting legacy. It defines how we live our lives. It transcends our goals.

Yet we also need to concentrate on these incremental goals, those smaller, paddling strokes" that are the building blocks of living a life of purpose. It's the combination of these two ends of the spectrumour vision of purpose and daily authentic actionthat enriches our lives. It's the focus, the visualization, the intention we put forth every day that adds depth and significance to our time here on earth.

In today's hectic world, our focus gets blurred easily and often. People, circumstances, stress and major life events distort the view. We flounder trying to get ourselves back in alignment. But more often than not, we get stuck.

On a solo paddle recently, I entered into a branch of the Trout River in northern Wisconsin that I have paddled many times. The water levels were extremely low and after going around a bend or two, I found myself stuck in an inch of water and mud. I could go no further down a river I normally paddle for a few miles.

So, being of contemplative spirit that morning, I took a break, sipped my coffee and lingered there awhile, marveling at the beauty surrounding me, listening to the morning calls of the wood ducks and Canadian geese and breathing in the fresh pine-scented air. I decided I liked being stuck. My focus shifted from paddling to just being there, relishing all the natural gifts of a cool summer morning.

After a while, I realized that if I was to get "unstuck," I needed to shift my focus and take some action. It was a small effort, a bit of work with my paddle in the mud, but I got moving again.

I thought about how often and easily we find ourselves stuck in life's seemingly endless ruts. We look around and perhaps enjoy the view, but soon we realize we need to get moving. We often lack the understanding of our next steps, so we remain stuck. That morning on the water reminded me that putting immediate focus on one small action to restart gets the momentum going. Soon I was out of the mud and paddling again.

Being stuck reminds me of a wonderful quote by one of my favorite authors, Dr. Wayne Dyer. He often says, 'Change the way you look at things, and the things you look at change." It's part of the universal Law of attraction—what you focus your thoughts on will manifest in your life. It's a powerful thing, focus.

This thought takes me back to the history of the kayak. At one time, the kayak did not exist. It was invented by the Inuit Peoples, who not only survived but thrived in the most adverse living conditions in the arctic. More out of necessity than pleasure, they had a thought, an idea of creating this mode of transportation. It took discipline, concentrated effort, a clear vision and focus to invent this simple vessel, the kayak. It became essential to their survival.

David W. Zimmerly, in an excerpt from *Qajaq, Kayaks of Siberia and Alaska,* writes, "The arctic kayak appeals to us on an emotional level beyond that inspired by more prosaic items of material culture. It has a romantic image associated with fur-clad Eskimos silently gliding along, hunting their sustenance or playing like otters in the waves; it illustrates the artistry and ingenuity of man in fashioning a superior means of transportation in an unforgiving climate. But perhaps we relate to the kayak on an even deeper level—it represents a means of man becoming at one with the rhythms of the sea; and as a means of transportation, it represents a singular image of freedom."

The simple, common purpose and remarkable focus of the Inuit people was to design a "superior means of transportation," but they created so much more. They gave us a gift beyond imagination. Their power of focus has clearly reached far beyond their original intention and leaves a lasting paddling legacy for all of us to enjoy.

So I challenge you now to focus on what resonates within you.

- *What do you care deeply about?*
- *What highest values give your life meaning?*
- *What one area of your life can you focus on to begin to manifest your deepest desires?*
- *What will really enhance the quality of your life?*
- *What is your lasting legacy?*

Freedom

Wild Rice Lake, Wisconsin

Freedom

"No man is free
who is not a master of himself."

~ Epictetus

Many times I have written in my paddling journal, "My kayak is my freedom." I used to feel the same way about riding my bike when I was younger. Funny how for me, on both land and water, the feeling of freedom comes from a very similar vehicle—a self-propelled, simple, solitary mode of transportation.

Slipping into the kayak and paddling away from the shore, an instant feeling of freedom overtakes me. The gentle push I give myself to get on the water is like a liberating nudge away from everything holding me back. The time on the water is an escape from life on land. Paddling away from my routine, I realize that nothing can really stop me from going forward, except myself.

Maybe it's the sense of self-sufficiency in paddling that brings forth this feeling of freedom. I paddle the kayak under my own power. I paddle on water hundreds of feet deep or six inches deep. I meander around river bends or venture out into the open water. I go as fast or as slow as I desire. I paddle in the pouring rain or in the warmth of the sunshine. I create my own experience, every time.

If freedom is defined as 'unrestricted use or access,' then kayaking for me is that freedom. A special peace of mind and confidence comes with the self-reliance of paddling. This feeling of autonomy heightens my awareness of the inherent knowledge that I am responsible for everything that happens to me on the water. r ecognizing this accountability and allowing it to absorb into the very core of my soul is one of the subtle freedoms that comes from spending time on the water. There are no accidents. Every decision I make has an impact on the quality of my paddling trip. Even outside forces that I cannot control—the weather, other boaters, unforeseen mishapsgive me the unbridled freedom to choose my response.

So it is true in our lives. Once we realize that we are responsible and accountable for every person, every thing, and every circumstance in our lives, we are no longer bound. Good or bad feelings, successful or unsuccessful occurrences, happy or sad times, we own them all. The feeling of freedom that emerges from this realization is both liberating and frightening. It is liberating because we have the freedom to choose our direction from this moment on. It is frightening because it means we have to do something about our place in life. We cannot blame others. If we don't accept accountability for everything in our lives, we will never grow or change or heal. Day after day, year after year, we will stagnate like a pond that has no water flowing in or out, and watch our dreams erode. One day, we will look back and ask ourselves, "How could I have done this to myself?"

Paddling allows me the freedom of time to think my own thoughts, to ponder life's bigger questions and to get clear about the path of my life. It allows for the emergence of the "aha" moments, when in a quiet space of time, I get real about the life I want to live. And I recognize that I have the freedom to create that life for myself.

But I must be willing. In kayaking, I must be willing to overcome any fears I might have about being on the water, or ending up in the water. I must be willing to endure some uncomfortable circumstances or inclement weather. I must be willing to paddle long stretches without rest or bathroom breaks. I must be willing to say "yes" to the experience. This unrestricted willingness is a freedom to open myself to the many special gifts I unexpectedly receive while paddling along.

In life, we also must be willing. The only way to reach new heights and live our best lives is to allow our spirits to be free and willing. By giving ourselves permission to get out of our ruts and look around, we might be surprised at the view. We might be inspired to discover the endless opportunities waiting to be seized. We might finally pry ourselves away from old beliefs and discover a new paradigm—one that is refreshing and unique—the freedom to live our lives authentically.

- *What are you willing to say "yes" to that you have put aside in the past?*

- *Are you willing to be honest about where your life is right now, and where you want it to go?*

- *Are you willing to discover the new "freedoms" that are waiting for you?*

- *Freedom means different things to different people. What does freedom mean to you?*

Solitude

Columbia Glacier, Prince William Sound, Alaska

Solitude

"Wilderness can be appreciated only by contrast,
and solitude understood only when
we have been without it."

~ Sigurd F. Olson

There are many "calls" that we reference in our lives: "the call of the wild"; "the call to a certain vocation"; "the call to serve". For me in my kayak, it is the "call to solitude" that beckons me.

In and of itself, solitude is a wonderful experience – that sense of enveloping silence that quiets my soul. I appreciate Sigurd Olson's quote about understanding solitude when I've been without it. When I've spent countless busy days scattering about with people, activities and my never-ending 'to-do' list, I begin to recognize that I ache for the solitude that brings me back to center and renders me whole.

Paddling alone, I can feel the peacefulness of solitude wrapping itself around me. In solitude, I may hear the soft voice of inspiration, clarify a deeper truth or revisit my priorities. I may restore my tired self or find a new beginning. But solitude's greatest blessing to me as I quietly paddle in my little red kayak is the gift of healing.

I have often written in my kayaking journal, that in the solitude of being on the water, early in the morning as the sun burns the night's fog away, that I can actually "feel my soul heal." I often paddle to a quiet space, rest my paddle atop the kayak and close my eyes. In the warm rays of the early morning sun, I sit in utter solitude and soak in its healing rays as though I am a dry human sponge longing to be filled with its nourishing waters.

I heal from the hectic pace of everyday life, which fragments my soul with its constant busyness. I heal from past experiences that need to be acknowledged and let go. I heal old emotions and mend broken relationships. I heal from deep loss and process my grief. Most importantly, I heal to allow myself the gift of going back to my life a better, more complete, compassionate person. There is a wonderful book written by Stephen Arterburn called *Healing is a Choice*. In it, he writes, "Healing is a choice. It is the choice to connect." In my kayak on the water, my choice is solitude — to heal, to grow and to reconnect with myself.

The solitude I find in kayaking is a treasured oasis of silence. To surround myself with silence, or rather have the silence surround me, is to stand back from the tapestry that is my life and more clearly see the whole picture. I come to know myself a little better with each trip into the waters of solitude. I come to understand how necessary it is for me to paddle away from life on the shore to a place of renewal and nourishment. Henry David Thoreau once said, "I come to my solitary woodland walk as the homesick go home." I, too, come to the shore with my kayak and paddle, homesick for time on the water where the gifts of solitude await me.

I learn from the birds and the animals and the elements of nature that I see on my paddling journeys. The majestic bald eagle soars above the long tree line, alone in the sky that is his domain. The great blue heron flees her post on the river's shore as I paddle by, for I have disturbed her solitude and she leaves to seek it again. The "busy beaver" works alone to build his intricate lodge along the river bank in his own rhythm of solitude. The lone deer enjoys her cool drink of water, eyeing me cautiously while savoring her little slice of solitude. Even the sun shines alone.

The most majestic journey into solitude was paddling through the icebergs at the edge of Columbia Glacier in Prince William Sound, Alaska in mid-June. Though paddling in a double kayak with "Mary" Jan and being with other kayakers on this adventure, an incredible feeling of "ice-olation" and solitude around these 'bergs permeated through my very core. I felt like we were the only people on earth. Our guide, Gunner, cautioned us not to get too close to these unwelcoming, deep blue icebergs, as chunks of ice could either fall off the top or break away underneath and pop up too close to us. He told us to never lose sight of one another, for in the maze of the icebergs, one could easily become disoriented. We heard the haunting, indescribable noise of the ice calving and then the unsettling silence that follows. I wrote in my journal at the end of that day, "Paddling around the icebergs gave me the surreal, eerie feeling of being on another planet." It was the adventure of a lifetime. Solitude supreme!

Experiencing solitude in my kayak on the water is transforming for me. Through the experience of solitude, I can start anew. As Mahatma Gandhi once wrote, "The soul requires inward restfulness to attain its full height." In this richness of "inward restfulness" I relish the rewards of solitude.

I think the early explorers and paddlers knew and understood the value of solitude. How else could they have been so daring, so adventurous, so willing to trust their instincts without the inner 'knowing' that comes from solitude? Free from the judgment and the opinions of others and the demands and habits of society, they were able to let the clarity that comes from solitude shine through on their journeys.

In our lives, it is often difficult to carve out large blocks of time for solitude. Our challenge lies in our ability and commitment to take time for a small slice every day. It may be rising earlier for meditation time, or taking a contemplative walk alone at the end of a busy day. However short our time, solitude is necessary to maintain our center and retain our wholeness.

Creating our solitude time is not always easy, because time alone is not something that is valued in our society. In her classic book, *Gift from the Sea* originally published in 1955, Anne Morrow Lindbergh wrote, "If one sets aside time for a business engagement, a trip to the hairdresser, a social engagement or a shopping expedition, that time is accepted as inviolable. But if one says: I cannot come because that is my hour to be alone; one is considered rude, egotistical or strange. What a commentary on our civilization, when being alone is considered suspect; when one has to apologize or it, make excuses, hide the fact that one practices it — like a secret vice!" Fifty-five years later, her timeless wisdom remains true today.

So I ask you:

- *How can you create a space in your daily life for solitude?*

- *When can you find the time to nourish your soul and rest your spirit?*

- *What dreams are lying dormant, waiting to come alive in the space of solitude?*

- *What new beginnings are beckoning?*

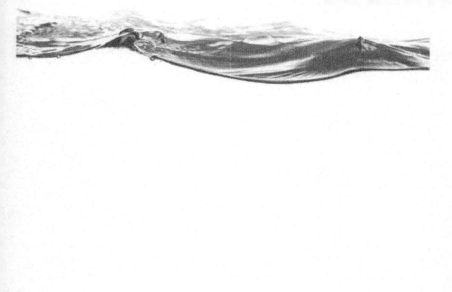

Clarity

Castle Rock Lake, Wisconsin

Clarity

"In one drop of water
we find all the secrets of the ocean."

~ Kahlil Gibran

I live in a place where the lakes become frozen tundra in winter. Like a bear that hibernates, I must put my paddle to rest. Water, the ever changing element, once again transforms itself into something different. A new season challenges me to hunker down and be content until I can kayak again.

So when spring arrives, the first paddle of the year is always very special. All winter I have so much "wanting" to be on the water, that when I finally go, a gate inside unlocks and I feel as though I could paddle forever. I push away from the shore, close my eyes, inhale deeply and an indescribable feeling comes over me like a breath of fresh spring air. It's as though my soul comes alive once again on the water and a time for rebirth and new beginnings has begun.

This rite of spring offers me an unspoiled opportunity for clarity. I feel the slate has been cleared with the harshness of winter. One of the reasons I journal, especially when I paddle, is because writing brings clarity to my thinking and the blank pages of the journal allow me a space to fully express my feelings, uninhibited by others' thoughts and opinions. Putting pen to paper illuminates my perspective.

While paddling in the early morning in the spring in Wisconsin, I often find remnants of winter. Ice clings to the low hanging branches on the shoreline, stubbornly resisting the seasonal transition. The air is cooler and often there is a mysterious mist and fog hovering over the water. This is a time of true adventure, a word that contains the noun 'advent,' which means a "beginning" or an "arrival."

Paddling in the fog is a wondrous experience. Like heading out into pea soup. no clear path, no clear vision, yet I paddle on, trusting in the journey and yielding to the experience. no clarity here. Sometimes, I can see just far enough to keep my bearings about my location on the lake. Other times, I have no clue how far I've paddled or exactly where I am. I momentarily feel lost, but then I remember the line from Joan anderson's book, *A Year by the Sea*. In it she writes, 'It occurs to me that being in the fog does not have to mean being altogether lost."

Often in life I feel the same. Life can be a little hazy. Sometimes the way is clouded, unclear and everywhere I turn, it looks the same. I feel lost in the fog of the constant choices and endless decisions to be made, often unsure of the next steps. I long for the clarity to know my direction, for the misty veil to lift and clear the way.

Paddling teaches me that there are two ways to attain clarity. In my kayak, if I paddle along in the fog, I may reach an unintended destination. This arrival is not a bad thing, as it offers the opportunity for new experiences and fresh challenges. The destination may not be what I had intended or what I had envisioned, but exciting nonetheless. Clarity often presents itself in these unexpected ways, coming in what we call the "aha" moments. An uncharted arrival at a place refreshingly unfamiliar.

The other path to clarity I discovered, which is really not a path, is to just be still and be present in the moment. I stay in the fog, relishing this sense of bewilderment. Slowly, the warmth of the sun clears the hazy mist, shedding light on my location. Even familiar surroundings somehow look different. I point my compass in a new direction, continue on and I am grateful for this advent of clarity, arriving on its own terms. A challenge in patience offering its own gratifying rewards.

I recently was blessed with the gift of an unexpected trip to the Caribbean with my dear, lifelong friend, Mary Kay Walsh. I have always wanted to paddle on water so clear that it appears the kayak is suspended in air. Now I had my chance. The kayaks available were sit-on-tops. I did not sit inside, but totally exposed on top of the kayak. Another distinctive characteristic of this kayak is a Plexiglas oval on the bottom allowing me to look down in to the crystal clear waters of the Great Bay. Talk about clarity. Even in 30 feet of water I could see to the bottom of the ocean and observe the vibrantly colored fish and the many species of coral. Paddling here proved to be a never-ending challenge to watch where I was going, because I was so enthralled with looking down below.

This unique paddling experience brings me full circle in my thoughts on clarity. The stunningly clear blue waters in the Caribbean are transparent, which is another word for clarity. That which is transparent allows objects to be seen clearly through it, according to *Roget's Thesaurus*.

Isn't clarity the ability to see through things so that their deeper meaning becomes evident?

- *So I challenge you now, to think of those parts of your life that are muddied and hazy.*

- *How do they impact your journey and what choices can you make to clear them up?*

- *If you could pick one area of your life where you crave clarity, what would it be and how can you lift your own foggy veil?*

Reflection

Trout River, Wisconsin

Motivation

Reflection

"A man sees in the world
what he carries in his heart."
- Johann Wolfgang van Goethe

Since this book is titled *Reflections from the Red Kayak*, I wanted the last section to be about reflection. In *Roget's Thesaurus*, similar words for reflection include thought, consideration, thinking, pondering, meditation and musing. Throughout my reflections in this book, I have provided some insights that hopefully help you to journal your own thoughts during your time on the water.

In this section I ponder another phrase for the word reflection, and that is mirror image. Of the four natural elements–water, air, fire and wind–water is the only element that is capable of providing a reflection. On my many solo journeys, this concept of reflection has fascinated me. I look out when the water is still and see the reflection of what is most immediate in my view. I marvel at how the reflection is exactly the same as the image. In studying these reflections, I have come to see them as my teachers.

When I look at a birch tree on the shoreline, hovering over the water, and then I look at its reflection, what do I see? I see the birch tree exactly as it is. I don't look at the reflection and see an aspen tree or an oak or an evergreen. I see a birch tree. It cannot be any other way.

Which leads me to these questions: In my life, how does the energy I send out come back to me? Do my thoughts, actions, and words reflect back to me in the same exact way I send them out? If I express anger and hatred, how can I expect joy and love to flow to me? Can my words and deeds return differently? That would violate one of the universal laws of nature and that is the "Law of Giving," which Deepak Chopra so magnificently outlines in his book, *The Seven Spiritual Laws of Success*. He notes that we are always in a dynamic exchange with the universe. nothing is static. He makes this law sound so easy as he writes, "Practicing the 'Law of Giving' is actually very simple: if you want joy, give joy to others; if you want love, learn to give love; if you want attention and appreciation, learn to give attention and appreciation.". and on it goes. He reminds us that it is the intention behind our giving that is most important. We may know it better as "what goes around, comes around."

I am starting to call this my "Law of the Birch Tree." To keep the lesson with me, I take myself back to my kayak and the reflection of the birch tree on the water, and think about how it could possibly reflect back as an aspen tree. What an absurd concept! It's really no different in my life. I am a product of nature and the natural laws apply to me, too.

I then took this concept of reflection one step further. I can put my paddle in the water and create a small ripple. Or the wind blows softly and small waves appear. These changes in the water now blur the reflection of the birch tree. It is still the birch tree, but it somehow appears different–wavy and indistinct. Other times when the wind is strong, causing the water to be choppy, the reflection of the birch tree is barely visible. It is still there, but completely distorted by the strong movement of the water.

How does this now apply to my life? I think sometimes my challenge is to gain a clear understanding of myself, my feelings, emotions and actions. If these are choppy, then it may not be immediately apparent to me that I project one thing, but think it is something else. Or maybe I put something out there and secretly expect something else in return. Often in times of stress or confusion, the reflection becomes distorted. The "Law of the Birch Tree" teaches me to recognize the reciprocity of life and keep my reflection clear.

Which brings me to a final insight on reflection. My outer world is a reflection of my inner world. The birch tree is the birch tree inside and out. So if my inner world is filled with anxiety, fear and chaos, then my outer world——my home, my relationships, my every day life——will be negatively affected. But if I am peaceful and calm, then my outer world will reflect tranquility and harmony. For me it's all about being authentic. And that is what I desire from my reflections of the birch tree. Mahatma Gandhi said it simply, "Be the change you want to see in the world."

So, if I want to see love, I must give love. If I want to have joy, I must be joyful. If I want peace, then I must be peaceful. I will let the world reflect back to me all the goodness I can give. I will be the birch tree!

Please take some time to reflect.

- *What type of energy do you bring to your life, and what do you expect in return?*

- *What can you change within you, right now, to reflect back more of what you want in life?*

- *What is your outer world saying about your inner world at this moment?*

Parting Thoughts

DuPage River, Illinois

The Reflections from the Red Kayak series was born out of a journey of healing on the water. An insightful inner journey to find authenticity, the series encourages others to embark on the same. Thought provoking questions at the end of each essay allow readers to journal their own thoughts and reflections.

All three books from the
Reflections from the Red Kayak series are
Available on Amazon.com.

- *Reflections from the Red Kayak: Thoughts on Life*
- *A Season on the Water: Reflections from the Red Kayak*
- *Change: Our Ever-Present Companion: Reflections from the Red Kayak*

For more information or to sign up for our inconsistent and irregular newsletter, please visit our website at www.redkayak.net.

Thank you, and keep paddlin' on...

Parting Thoughts

"Everybody needs beauty as well as bread,
places to play in and pray in,
where nature may heal and
give strength to body and soul."

~ John Muir

Before paddling today on this cool, crisp Wisconsin morning, I read a saying taken from *A Course in Miracles* as published in a Helen exley Gift book titled, *... And Wisdom Comes Quietly.* It goes like this —"There is a silence into which the world cannot intrude. There is an ancient peace you carry in your heart and have not lost."

As I read and re-read these lines, the words 'ancient peace' resonated in my soul. For me, that is the essence of paddling; the restoration of my own ancient peace in the "silence the world cannot intrude." As I paddled quietly on the calm waters of Wild rice Lake this morning, I opened my heart to the presence of ancient peace:

> Thinking about the early explorers like Lewis and Clark and their many expeditions takes me back to ... ancient peace.

> As I dipped my paddle end over end to my own rhythm, it flowed through me ... ancient peace.

> From the soft morning breeze bringing gentle ripples to the water, it touched me ... ancient peace.

> In the distant, haunting call of the common loon, I heard the sound of ... ancient peace.

> Seeing the shimmering reflection of the birch trees on the water, I witnessed ... ancient peace.

Watching the majestic bald eagle lifting off from a branch high in the pine tree to soar in the sky, it stirred in me ... ancient peace.

In the clear blue sky briefly interrupted by puffy white clouds, it surrounded me ... ancient peace.

In the silence of the woods and water, it returned to me ... ancient peace.

May you find the "silence the world cannot intrude" on your paddling journeys. May ancient peace return to you.

"You cannot step into the same river twice.
Each time it is different,
and so are you."

-	Heraclitus

About the Author

Photo by Janie Ford

Mary Anne Smrz is a paddler, who uses insights gained on the water to enrich her own life and the lives of others. In her professional life, Mary Anne is a Certified Financial Planner® and works for a financial planning firm in Oak Brook, Illinois. She has received many prestigious awards as a financial advisor and is among a select group certified to teach financial wellness programs. In her life of outdoor passions, she kayaks, loves to spend time in nature and hikes with her yellow lab, Bayfield. She writes from her home in Wisconsin. The balance and focus she gains from being "of the water" enriches every facet of her life and career.

Photo by Janet Murawski